We're Going on a Bear Hunt

RE-PLAYED BY
VIVIAN FRENCH

FROM THE BOOK BY
MICHAEL ROSEN AND HELEN OXENBURY

WALKER BOOKS
AND SUBSIDIARIES

LONDON · BOSTON · SYDNEY · AUCKLAND

First published 2000 by Walker Books Ltd, 87 Vauxhall Walk, London SE11 5HJ

This edition published 2012

2 4 6 8 10 9 7 5 3 1

Playscript © 2000 Vivian French
Original text © 1989 Michael Rosen
Illustrations © 1989 Helen Oxenbury

The right of Vivian French, Michael Rosen and Helen Oxenbury to be identified as authors and illustrator respectively of this work has been asserted by them in accordance with the Copyright, Designs and Patents Act 1988

This book has been typeset in Stempel Schneidler

Printed in China

British Library Cataloguing in Publication Data:
a catalogue record for this book is available from the British Library

ISBN 978-1-4063-4333-5

www.walker.co.uk

Notes for Children

We're Going on a Bear Hunt is the story of a
scary day out for three children, a dad and a baby.
You may know the story already, but it doesn't
matter if you don't.

This book is a little different from other picture books.
You will be sharing it with other people and telling
the story together.

You can read

this line

this line

this line

or this line.

Even when someone else is reading, try to follow
the words. It will help when it's your turn!

We're going on a bear hunt.

A what hunt?

A where hunt?

We're going on a bear hunt.

And we're going to go today.

STOP!

What is it?

What's the matter?

Why are we stopping?

I don't want to go.

Why don't you want to go?

You're scared!

No, I'm not! I think it's going to rain.

No, it won't.

It's a beautiful day!

Shall I bring my umbrella?

You won't need it. Let's go!

We're going on a bear hunt.

We're going to catch a big one.

What a beautiful day!

We're not scared.

Uh-uh! Grass!

Long wavy grass.

We can't go over it.

We can't go under it.

Oh no! We've got to go through it!

STOP!

What is it?

There might be snakes.

OOOOOOOOOOOOOH!

There aren't any snakes.

Oh.

All right. Let's go.

Swishy swashy!

Swishy swashy!

SWISHY SWASHY!

We're going on a bear hunt.

We're going to catch a big one.

What a beautiful day!

We're not scared.

Uh-uh! A river!

A deep cold river.

We can't go over it.

We can't go under it.

Oh no! We've got to go through it!

Splash splosh!

Splash splosh!

SPLASH SPLOSH!

We're going on a bear hunt.

We're going to catch a big one.

What a beautiful day!

Stop!

What is it?

Mud!

Thick oozy mud.

Squelch squerch!

Squelch squerch!

SQUELCH SQUERCH!

I'm stuck!

Give me your hand.

And I'll hold yours.

And I'll hold yours.

Pull! Pull! Pull!

I've lost my boot.

Off we go again.

Where are we now?

We're down in a forest.

A big forest.

A very big forest.

A dark forest.

A very dark forest.

A big dark forest.

OOOOOOOOOOOOH!

Here we go.

Stumble trip!

Stumble trip!

STUMBLE TRIP!

We're going on a bear hunt.

We're going to catch a big one.

What a beautiful day!

We're not scared.

Uh-uh! A snowstorm!

A swirling whirling snowstorm.

Stop!

Why?

It's not a beautiful day.

It's snowing.

And we can't go over it.

We can't go under it.

We've got to go through it!

Hoooo woooo!

Hoooo woooo!

HOOOO WOOOO!

Whatever next?

A CAVE!

It's very dark.

It's very narrow.

It's very gloomy.

I think this is the wrong way.

Oh no it isn't!

Oh yes it is!

OH NO IT ISN'T!

Shhhhh!

Here we go.

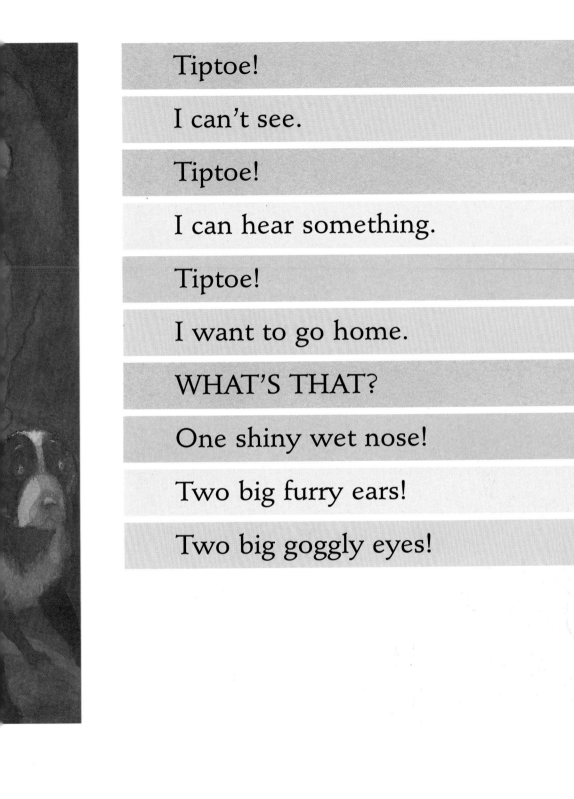

Tiptoe!

I can't see.

Tiptoe!

I can hear something.

Tiptoe!

I want to go home.

WHAT'S THAT?

One shiny wet nose!

Two big furry ears!

Two big goggly eyes!

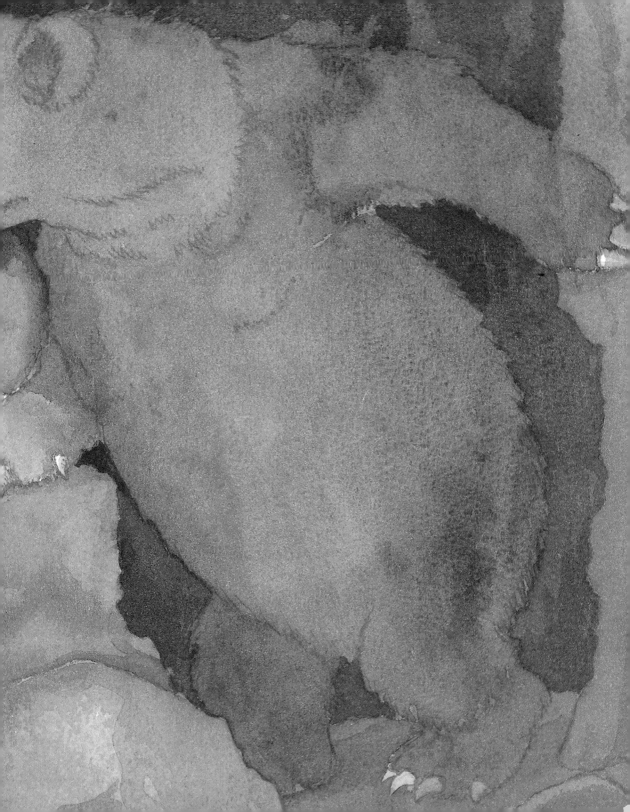

Quick! Back through the cave!

Tiptoe! Tiptoe!

Back through the snowstorm!

Hoooo woooo! Hoooo woooo!

Back through the forest!

Stumble trip! Stumble trip!

Back through the mud!

Squelch squerch! Squelch squerch!

Look! I've found my boot.

Back through the river!

Splash splosh! Splash splosh!

Back through the grass!

Swishy swashy! Swishy swashy!

Through the door –

And up the stairs.

Oh no!

We forgot to shut the door.

Back downstairs.

Shut the door.

Back upstairs.

Into the bedroom.

Into bed.

Under the covers.

We're not going on a bear hunt

EVER AGAIN!

Notes for Teachers

Story Plays are written and presented in a way that encourages children to read aloud together. They are dramatic versions of memorable and exciting stories, told in strongly patterned language which gives children the chance to practise at a vital stage of their reading development. Sharing stories in this way makes reading an active and enjoyable process, and one that draws in even the reticent reader.

The story is told by four different voices, divided into four colours so that each child can easily read his or her part. The blue line is for more experienced readers; the red line for less experienced readers. When there are more than four children in a group, there is an ideal opportunity for paired reading. Partnering a more experienced reader with a less experienced one can be very supportive and provides a learning experience for both children.

Story Plays encourage children to share in the reading of a whole text in a collaborative and interactive way. This makes them perfect for group and guided reading activities. Children will find they need to pay close attention to the print and punctuation, and to use the meaning of the whole story in order to read it with expression and a real sense of voice.